NATURAL WORLD

ZEBRA

HABITATS • LIFE CYCLES • FOOD CHAINS • THREATS

Malcolm Penny

HODDER
Wayland

an imprint of Hodder
Children's Books

WWF®

Produced in Association with WWF-UK

NATURAL WORLD

Chimpanzee • Crocodile • Black Rhino • Dolphin • Elephant • Giant Panda
Giraffe • Golden Eagle • Gorilla • Great White Shark • Grizzly Bear
Hippopotamus • Killer Whale • Koala • Leopard • Lion • Orangutan
Penguin • Polar Bear • Tiger • Wolf • Zebra

Produced for Hodder Wayland by
Roger Coote Publishing
Gissing's Farm, Fressingfield
Suffolk IP21 5SH, UK

Produced in association with WWF-UK.
WWF-UK registered charity number
1081247. A company limited by guarantee
number 4016725. Panda device © 1986 WWF.
® WWF registered trademark owner.

Cover: A zebra, up close.
Title page: Plains zebras are abundant in East Africa.
Contents page: A zebra's pattern is unique, like a human fingerprint.
Index page: Mountain zebras in southern Africa are the most endangered of
the three zebra species.

Published in Great Britain in 2002 by Hodder Wayland,
an imprint of Hodder Children's Books
Text copyright © 2002 Hodder Wayland
Volume copyright © 2002 Hodder Wayland
This paperback edition published in 2002

Editor: Steve Parker
Series editor: Victoria Brooker
Designer: Victoria Webb

British Library Cataloguing in Publication Data
Penny, Malcolm
Zebra. - (Natural World)
1.Zebras - Juvenile literature
I.Title
599.6'657

ISBN 0 7502 3996 4

Printed and bound by G. Canale & C.S.p.A., Turin, Italy

Hodder Children's Books
A division of Hodder Headline Limited
338 Euston Road, London NW1 3BH

Picture acknowledgements
Bruce Coleman Collection front cover Trevor Barrett,
11 Staffan Widstrand, 14 Gunter Kohler, 16 Natural
Selection Inc, 23 Christer Fredriksson, 29 Sarah Cook,
42 Staffan Widstrand, 44 middle Staffan Widstrand,
45 top Gunter Kohler, 45 bottom Sarah Cook; *Corbis*
15 Wolfgang Kaehler, 28 Karl Ammann; *Digital Vision*
1, 8, 9, 20, 33, 34, 43; *FLPA* 3 Martin Withers, 7 W
Wisniewski, 10 Terry Andrewartha, 12 W Wisniewski,
18 A Wharton, 21 Philip Perry, 22 W Wisniewski, 24
Gerard Lacz, 25 W Wisniewski, 26-7 David Hosking,
31 F Hartmann, 36 Minden Pictures, 38 Leonard Lee
Rue, 41 Martin Withers, 44 top Terry Andrewartha,
44 bottom W Wisniewski; *NHPA* 13 Julie Meech, 27
Daryl Balfour, 37 Anthony Bannister, 48 Nigel J
Dennis; *Oxford Scientific Films* 17 John Downer, 30
Steve Turner, 39 Steve Turner, 40 Konrad Wothe; *Still
Pictures* 6 M&C Denis-Huot, 32 M&C Denis-Huot, 35
M&C Denis-Huot, 45 middle M&C Denis-Huot.
Artwork by Michael Posen.

Contents

Meet the Zebra

No other animals look like zebras. They are very similar to horses, but they have a unique coat pattern of black and white stripes. There are three kinds, or species, of zebras. All live in Africa. Only the plains zebra is still fairly common. The other two species, Grevy's zebra and the mountain zebra, are much rarer.

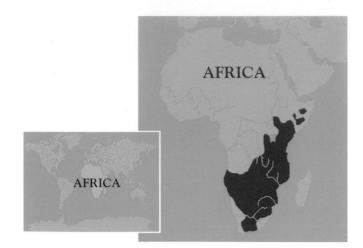

▲ The red shading shows where zebras live. Plains zebras are found in East Africa. Mountain zebras live in Southern and South-West Africa. Grevy's zebras live in Ethiopia, Somalia and northern Kenya. The inset map shows where Africa is.

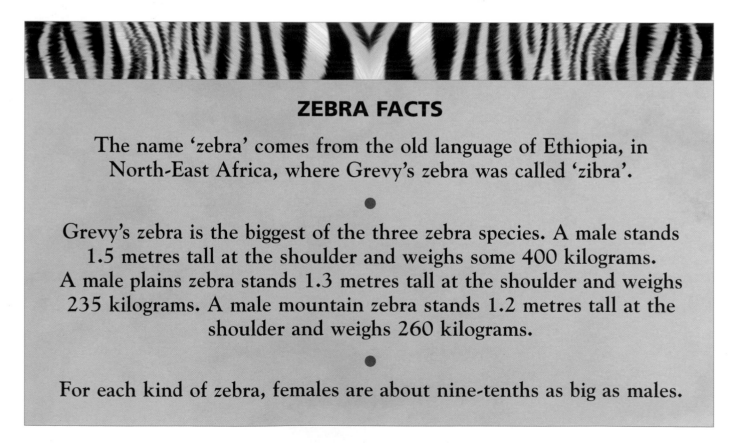

ZEBRA FACTS

The name 'zebra' comes from the old language of Ethiopia, in North-East Africa, where Grevy's zebra was called 'zibra'.

•

Grevy's zebra is the biggest of the three zebra species. A male stands 1.5 metres tall at the shoulder and weighs some 400 kilograms. A male plains zebra stands 1.3 metres tall at the shoulder and weighs 235 kilograms. A male mountain zebra stands 1.2 metres tall at the shoulder and weighs 260 kilograms.

•

For each kind of zebra, females are about nine-tenths as big as males.

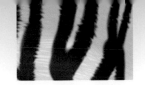

Ears
The long, sensitive ears can move easily to find the direction of a faint sound.

Eyes
The eyes are set high on the sides of the head. They can see all around to spot danger, even while the zebra feeds head-down.

Stripes
Each species of zebra has a different overall stripe pattern. But even in the same species, no two zebras have exactly the same stripes. They are all different, like our fingerprints. The stripes are mainly up-and-down on the body and ringed around the legs.

Nose
The large snout gives the zebra a very keen sense of smell.

Mouth
The zebra's long jaws have sharp front teeth for cropping or cutting off grass, and broad, powerful back teeth for grinding it. The front teeth are also used as weapons when fighting.

Legs
The zebra's long, slender legs allow it to run fast in open country.

Hooves
Like a horse, a zebra only has one toe on each foot. This has a hard, tough hoof at the end. Zebras kick with their hooves while fighting or in self defence.

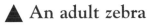 An adult zebra

Habitat

Each species of zebra lives in a slightly different habitat. Plains zebras prefer savannah, where scattered trees on the grassy plains provide shade during the hot day. Mountain zebras live in a similar habitat in Southern Africa, but higher up in the hills, where it is cooler. Grevy's zebras are found in much drier, almost desert-like habitats of grass and scrub.

▼ Plains zebras in the wide grasslands of Amboseli National Park, with Mount Kilimanjaro in the background.

LONG-GONE ZEBRA

The Cape quagga was a type of zebra from Southern Africa. It was yellow-brown, with stripes only on its head, neck and shoulders. Quaggas were shot by farmers who wanted to take the grasslands for their cattle. The last quagga died in 1874 in Amsterdam Zoo, in the Netherlands. The species is now extinct (gone for ever).

In northern Kenya, the southern edge of the Grevy's zebra range overlaps with the northern edge of the plains zebra range. So the two species sometimes meet.

In tropical Africa, long dry periods are followed by spells of heavy rain. Zebras must travel great distances to find food and water in the dry season. They come together in large groups called herds. This helps to keep them safe from enemies. Older, more experienced zebras lead the herds and show the others where to find water and fresh grass.

▲ Zebras can reach speeds of 60-70 kilometres per hour.

Neighbours

The zebras usually seen in books, films and
television programmes are plains zebras. They
share the grasslands and waterholes with many
other large plant-eaters. These friendly
neighbours include giraffes, wildebeest and
other antelopes, and gazelles like the Thomson's
gazelle. Zebras usually stay together in their
own group, but they graze or drink near to
these other plant-eaters.

Other neighbours are not so friendly. Lions and
hyenas hunt zebras, mainly at night. But they
may attack a zebra by day, when it comes to
drink at a waterhole.

▲ The waterhole is a
daily meeting place for
African animals.

▶ Distant cousins:
this white rhino and
her calf look very
different from zebras,
but they are related.

Relatives

Another neighbour that grazes alongside the zebra is the rhinoceros. In fact, the rhino and zebra are more than neighbours – they are relatives. They belong to a large group of mammals called the odd-toed ungulates. This means they have an odd number of toes on each foot, and each toe is tipped with a hoof. Also in the group are horses and asses, which are the zebra's closest relatives, and tapirs.

OTHER NAMES

The plains zebra is sometimes called the common or Burchell's zebra. Its scientific name is *Equus burchelli*. Grant's zebra is a subspecies of this species.

●

Grevy's zebra is sometimes known as the imperial zebra. Its scientific name is *Equus grevyi*.

●

The mountain zebra's scientific name is *Equus zebra*.

A Zebra is Born

A young zebra is called a foal. Most foals are born after the rainy season has started. This date varies in different parts of Africa. In East African countries such as Kenya and Tanzania, where plains zebras live, the rainy season is between January and March.

▼ A plains zebra mother with her newborn foal in the Maasai Mara nature reserve, Kenya. The foal's father is not far away.

SIZE AT BIRTH

For the plains zebra, a male foal weighs about 33 kilograms. A female foal is slightly smaller at 31 kilograms.

The mother zebra, or mare, is pregnant (expecting a baby) for almost exactly a year. One day she lies down on her side and gives birth to a single foal. This happens very quickly. The father zebra, the stallion, stands guard close by. The new foal has much longer hair than an adult zebra. Also its stripes are brown. They will turn black when the foal is about four months old.

Some baby animals are helpless when they are born. But baby zebras must be able to travel with the family as soon as possible. Within 15-20 minutes of birth, a zebra foal can stand and walk. After just one hour it is feeding on its mother's milk.

▶ Still damp after being born, a zebra foal stands unsteadily for the first time.

◀ Grant's zebra is a subspecies of plains zebra. This mother will protect her foal against all other animals.

Back with the family

For the first few days, the mother zebra chases away any animal that comes within a few metres of her baby. This includes even its father, the stallion. During this time, the newborn zebra learns to recognize and follow the first moving thing it sees – its mother. This is called 'imprinting'. Many young animals do it. Imprinting makes sure that the baby knows and follows only its mother, who will feed and protect it.

TWIN DANGERS

The two main risks for a young zebra are lack of food, and enemies such as big cats. In some years, for every three foals born, two die in their first few weeks.

▼ Hyenas used to be thought of as scavengers, but now they are known to be active and successful hunters.

A few days later the mother zebra allows other herd members to come near. They get to know the new baby and groom it by gently nibbling its shoulders and neck. Imprinting means that, even in the middle of the busy zebra herd, the baby knows its mother.

Life is always dangerous for zebras – especially for young foals. There are predators such as lions and hyenas. Also, if the rains fail, food becomes scarce. The zebra mother cannot make enough milk to feed her baby, and the foal may die.

Growing up

The mother zebra grooms her foal regularly, sometimes for half an hour at a time. She gently nibbles its fur, especially around the neck and shoulders, and back over the body. Grooming is very important among zebras, when they are young and also when they are grown up. It keeps them together as family members, as well as getting rid of pests such as flies.

The foal feeds on its mother's milk, but it can nibble grass after only one week. Its weight increases by half a kilogram each day. Between two and three months of age, it is weaned – it no longer takes milk, and eats only plant food.

◄ For the first two or three months, its mother is the foal's main source of food.

▲ African wild dogs are very successful hunters in packs. This is a group of pups.

ZEBRAS AT PLAY

Zebra foals are very playful. They race and chase with each other, and practise grooming. They also play with other young animals such as antelopes and gazelles. Young male zebras pretend to fight each other from a very early age.

Zebras fight fiercely against predators. A pack of African wild dogs might surround the mother, her new foal and her older offspring. The mother and offspring will battle to keep the dogs away from the foal. Soon the rest of their group gallop up, to surround and protect them. Then they all race away.

Learning to Survive

The young zebra must stay with its herd, not only to find food and water, but to be safe from predators. If there is any threat, one herd member is likely to notice. Then all the members watch, listen and sniff the air, ready to run.

Sometimes, as zebras drink at a waterhole, they seem to panic for no reason. They jump about and mill around in a cloud of dust, then settle down again. Perhaps one of them heard a noise. Perhaps they are letting predators know that they are alert.

▲ Plains zebras in the Okavango Delta, Botswana, run from the photographer's aircraft.

FAST ESCAPE

On land, zebras can run faster and further than most of their enemies. They can reach speeds of 60-70 kilometres per hour. But in the water, they are at the mercy of crocodiles.

Zebras and wildebeest often travel in long, straggling columns. Such huge herds attract hungry predators. The herd members look out for each other and protect each other. But there is one part of the long journey, or migration, where they have no protection. Most migrations start during the rainy season, when rivers are full of water. The zebras must cross rivers to reach fresh grazing. Many are pulled under as they swim through the swirling waters – by crocodiles.

▼ Dangerous times: a mixed herd of zebras and wildebeest cross the Mara River, Kenya. The crocodiles have been waiting for them.

Feeding

Zebras are grazers – they eat grass and other ground plants. Grass is easy to find, but it is difficult to eat and digest (break down inside the body). It is very hard and wears away the teeth. Zebras have special ridges on their teeth to reduce this wear, as they chew and grind up the grass.

▲ Grevy's zebras in northern Kenya can live well on dry grass, selecting the best plants with their sensitive lips.

To digest the tough grass, zebras have tiny helpers. These are microscopic living things called bacteria, inside their bodies. The chewed grass passes into a large, bag-shaped part of the zebra's gut, called the caecum. The bacteria work on the grass using powerful juices, in a process called fermentation. When the food is broken down, the zebra can take the nutrients into its body.

ZEBRA FOOD CHAIN

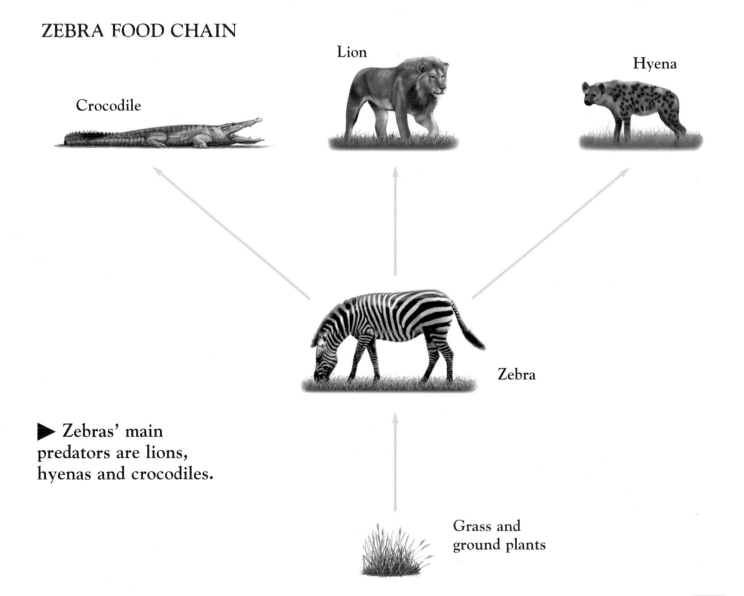

Crocodile

Lion

Hyena

Zebra

▶ Zebras' main predators are lions, hyenas and crocodiles.

Grass and ground plants

The search for water

Zebras must drink water every day. In dry weather they need to walk further, not only for fresh grass, but to find a well-filled waterhole. Older members of the herd remember places where grass and water are near each other.

However, taking a drink is always dangerous. Predators such as lions know that zebras need water each day. They wait by a waterhole, ready to pounce. The zebras have a terrible choice. They can risk dying of thirst, or becoming a lion's lunch.

▼ Ears pricked and eyes wide open, drinking zebras are alert for danger.

20

Zebras defend themselves by kicking and biting. But they prefer to detect danger early, and run away using their great speed and stamina, rather than fight. Zebras like to drink when there are other animals at the waterhole. They can all watch, listen and sniff for predators. When one detects danger, it alerts the others by its sounds or actions. Baboons, in particular, react noisily if a predator comes near. This warns all the creatures at the waterhole, and they leap up and race away in a cloud of dust.

▼ A lioness watches a waterhole from a distance. The zebras are watching her, and will run if she comes too close.

Why are zebras striped?

Zebras may be striped for a number of reasons. The stripes may confuse predators. They make it difficult for a lion to single out an individual zebra from the milling herd. But lions seem to kill zebras easily and often. So this cannot be the main reason.

Another idea is that stripes attract zebras to each other so they always come together into a crowd. This is much safer than being alone or widely spaced. Also each pattern of stripes is different for each zebra. So herd members may recognize each other by their patterns.

▲ Chapman's zebra, another subspecies of plains zebra, often has an almost solid black back.

The stripes are certainly not for camouflage, even in tall grass. Out on the plains, zebras show up very clearly. They make no attempt to hide from predators. They stand around in the open, in noisy, bustling groups.

The truth is that scientists do not really know why zebras have stripes. They have suggested many possible reasons but there doesn't seem to be a single, clear answer. Perhaps it is a mixture of reasons.

▼ How many zebras in this picture? A lion would find it hard to choose one to attack.

Adult Life

Plains zebras live in family groups. Each is led by a dominant male, the stallion. His group contains about six females. These stay with him throughout their adult lives. Each female usually produces a foal every two years. The stallion guards his family carefully, and brings back any members who wander off. Mountain zebras also live in family groups, like the plains zebras.

▼ When young males practise fighting, it can look serious, but it is only play.

Each zebra family group has an area called its home range. This usually overlaps the home ranges of neighbouring groups. In good grassland where food is plentiful, a home range may be about 80 square kilometres. Where the grass is poor, it may be four or five times larger.

As young zebras grow up, they leave their family. Young males are forced out by the stallion when they reach about four years of age and begin to threaten his dominant position. These young males join together in bachelor groups, where they practise fighting. As they gain in strength and experience, some gather groups of their own.

Female zebras are grown up at two years of age. They may join the family group of another stallion. Or several females may form a new group with a male from a bachelor group.

▲ A large herd of zebras is made up of many family groups. Each group has about 12 members – a stallion, his mares and their foals.

▲ Etosha National Park, Namibia, is perfect country for zebras. The wide open savannah gives them a good view of approaching danger.

In the herd

Zebras communicate with each other mainly by sounds and smells. When they sense danger, they make a barking noise that alerts the others. Young zebras scream if they are attacked, to bring nearby adults to their defence. When they drink at night, zebras are very noisy, so they know where they all are in the darkness.

THE HORSE FAMILY

Zebras and their close relatives, horses and asses, make up the animal family known as equids, Equidae. This contains three species of zebras, two species of wild asses, and two species of horse.

Male zebras recognize the sounds or 'voices' of their own family group, and also of other stallions which they have met in the past. This helps to reduce fighting. One male may remember that he lost the last battle to another male, so he avoids conflict. Often a stallion calls to another, and the two approach slowly until their noses touch. Then they rub their bodies together, perhaps to avoid a fight.

The scent of dung is another way of passing on information. Males all leave their dung in one place, forming a large communal pile. These piles are like a record or 'visitor's book' showing which males have passed by. Other males 'read the book' by smelling the pile, then adding to it themselves. This helps each male to keep track of rivals in the area.

▶ Touching their neck and back gives pleasure to all horses. They use it as a friendly greeting.

Fighting

Male zebras fight each other fiercely during the breeding season, as they try to gather females for their groups. From an early age they practise their fighting skills among themselves, first as foals and then in bachelor groups.

▼ You can tell that these young males are only play-fighting, because the standing one is not trying to get out of the way.

▲ Serious fights can go on for as long as an hour, and may cause serious injuries.

When fighting, the male zebra kicks out with his front hooves. But his main weapon is his teeth, and his main target is the opponent's front legs. A strong bite here can cripple the opponent and put an end to the battle. This is why fighting zebras often crouch down on their front knees, to protect their legs. Bites are also aimed at the opponent's sensitive rear end, neck and shoulders.

Both male and female zebras fight against predators. In a battle between a lion and a male Grevy's zebra, the two animals can kill each other. Sometimes a zebra can fight off as many as five attacking hyenas.

The unusual zebra

Grevy's zebra is rather different from the other two zebras. Its closest relatives are horses which once lived in South Africa and China, but which have died out. Also this zebra has a different form of social life from the other two.

A male Grevy's zebra does not gather a group of females. Instead he defends an area called a territory against rival males. A territory may be as big as 10 square kilometres. The male marks the boundaries with large piles of dung, which act as warnings to other males – keep out! Males which do not have a territory live in small bachelor groups.

FRENCH NAME

Grevy's zebra was discovered and described by scientists in 1882. It was named after the President of France at the time, Jules Grévy.

▼ Grevy's zebra has a narrow face and large, rounded ears. It is only distantly related to the other two zebra species.

CIRCUS ZEBRAS

In Ancient Rome, Grevy's zebra was trained as a circus animal. It was called *Hippotigris*, 'horse-tiger', because of its horse-like shape and tiger-like stripes.

▲ Grevy's zebra lives around the southern end of Lake Turkana, in northern Kenya, between the desert where the African wild ass lives, and the lush habitat of the plains zebra.

Female Grevy's zebras form wandering groups which pass through the territories of males. When the females are ready to breed, they mate with the male of the territory they are in. Then they leave to raise the young on their own.

The reason for this type of social life is shortage of food. There is not enough grass on the dry plains to support large groups of zebras. They have a better chance of finding enough to eat if they spread out.

Breeding Time

Zebras time their breeding season so that mares produce foals after the rains start. This makes sure there is plenty of grass to eat. A mare has her first foal at three or four years of age. A stallion cannot breed until he is big and strong enough to win a group of females, or for a Grevy's zebra, to establish a territory.

▲ A bachelor group of Grevy's zebras. Males cannot breed until they are at least 4-6 years old.

LONG LIFE

The most dangerous time for a zebra is the first few weeks of life. If it survives to adulthood, it may live to about 25 years of age.

▼ An older mare with her foal is secure as a member of a family group.

A young female zebra first comes into season (becomes ready to breed) at about two years old. But she does not mate this time. She 'advertises' by standing with her back legs apart and her tail raised. The nearby stallions soon notice and fight each other to gain her for their group.

Next year, when the female comes into season again, she is a permanent member of a group and ready to mate. Older females that have had foals do not 'advertise'. They are already members of a group, with just one stallion who is their only mate.

Courtship and mating

In each zebra family group, the stallion checks his mares carefully to find out when they are in season. In particular, he smells their urine to detect substances called hormones. To do this he raises his head and curls his lip so that the air passes over a sensitive part inside his nose. This action is called the flehmen response. When the stallion finds a female in season, courtship can begin.

▲ The flehmen response helps a stallion to detect the hormones in a female's urine.

The stallion follows the mare until she allows him to mate. When she produces droppings, he covers them with his own dung. This hides the scent of her hormones, which could otherwise attract nearby males.

Before mating takes place, the stallion nibbles gently at the mare's shoulders and neck. This is an adult version of the grooming behaviour between mothers and foals.

Mares come into season again very quickly after they have given birth. So it is possible for a mare to have a foal every year. But most mares take a year off to recover from the strain. They produce a foal every two years.

▼ Raising a foal is a very tiring year's work for its mother.

Threats

Zebras are in constant danger from predators such as lions, leopards, hyenas, African wild dogs and crocodiles. Another great threat is dry weather, which brings a shortage of drinking water. Lack of food is less serious because zebras survive by grazing dry, coarse grass that few other plant-eaters can consume. But they cannot get by without their daily drink.

▼ Closing in: a lioness prepares to pounce on a fleeing zebra.

► Bot-flies are parasites of many different animals. This one hatched from a larva found in the gut of an elephant.

DISEASES

Zebras suffer from a variety of diseases. These include redwater fever, which is carried by a small pest called a tick, and anthrax, which is spread by spores and kills many animals in the African bush.

Zebras are bitten by various small pests like fleas and ticks. A particularly painful pest is the bot-fly or warble-fly. It lays eggs on the zebra's legs and sides. The zebra licks off and swallows the eggs as it grooms itself. The eggs hatch inside the zebra, into grub-like larvae which suck the zebra's blood. They cause infection which can lead to severe pain and even death.

Zebras, like all members of the horse family, sense that the bot-fly means trouble. They run around in panic when these flies come near. But they have little chance of escape. The bot-fly buzzes along faster than any other insect, reaching speeds of 80 kilometres per hour.

Zebras and people

In many parts of the world, wild horses and their relatives disappeared long ago. Some were hunted as food or killed to prevent them breeding with domestic horses. Africa is the last stronghold for members of the horse family, and especially zebras. African people have always admired zebras for their beauty. The Maasai people like them for a more useful reason. Zebras eat tough, coarse grass, and this encourages the growth of young, fresh grass for the Maasai's cattle.

▲ Maasai tribesmen drive their cattle into an enclosure for the night.

PART OF NATURE

Zebras are an important part of the balance of nature. They graze grass and maintain the savannahs, and in turn, become food for predators. The numbers of zebras affect the numbers of lions, hyenas and other powerful hunters – the creatures that bring many visitors to Africa.

When European farmers arrived in Africa, they did not understand that zebras lived in balance with the grasslands. Many zebras were shot because they ate the food, and drank the water, which the farmers wanted for their own cattle. Zebras were also killed for their meat and for their beautifully patterned skins. These were made into clothes, bags and even furniture.

▼ A pile of wildlife trophies, including zebra skins, that were captured from poachers in Nairobi National Park, Kenya.

Zebras everywhere

Even when zebras were seen as pests and shot on sight, some people tried to protect them and make them useful. Many were sent to zoos and parks around the world. A few were even trained like horses to pull carts and traps. In the 1930s in Oxfordshire, England, the Duke of Marlborough drove a pony trap pulled by a pair of zebras. But this fashion soon died out, especially as cars became more popular.

▼ Far from home: a zebra in snow in a north European zoo.

The distinctive black and white stripes of the zebra have made its name common in many ways. It is often given to birds, fish, insects and other animals that happen to have a similar pattern. So there are zebra finches, zebra spiders, zebra danio fish and so on.

In Africa, a great tribute to the zebra is seen on the vehicles in wildlife parks and nature reserves. Many are painted with curved or wavy black and white stripes, in honour of the graceful wild horses that visitors come so far to see.

▲ The shot of a lifetime: a tourist bus on safari.

41

Conservation

At present, the plains zebra is not in great danger. Its numbers are reasonably large and stable. But mountain and Grevy's zebras are both under threat. They are protected by laws and in wildlife parks.

▲ Careful planning and protection is the best hope for Africa's zebras. These conservationists work in Selous National Park, Tanzania.

It is difficult to assess the numbers of Grevy's zebras, especially in the remote northern parts of its range. This species is still shot for its beautiful skin. The Galla people of Ethiopia have a tradition of using zebra manes to decorate the necks of their own horses. In northern Kenya, about 13,000 Grevy's zebras live in protected areas in Lake Turkana National Park. There is also a special reserve for them on the northern border of Kenya, at Rumuruti.

SYMBOL OF TOURISM

Many people now realize that zebras are worth much more alive than dead. They have become a symbol of the African savannah. Tourists who do not see zebras during their visit are usually very disappointed!

In the 1950s, the numbers of mountain zebras fell from about 70,000 to only 7,000. They are now protected in national parks in South Africa, where the herds are gradually recovering in size.

▼ Family album: zebras are the stars of most people's safari photo collections.

Zebra Life Cycle

 1 A female zebra gives birth to her foal after a pregnancy, or gestation period, of about 350 days (almost one year). In Grevy's zebra this time is slightly longer, nearer 400 days.

 **2** The new foal can stand up and walk after 20 minutes. It feeds on its mother's milk after about one hour.

 **3** For the first few days, the mother keeps all other animals away from her foal, including other zebras. Then members of her family group are allowed to lick and groom the baby.

 **4** Zebra foals double their birth weight after one month, to 60-70 kilograms. They are weaned (stop taking mother's milk) after about three months.

 **5** At two years of age, a young female zebra leaves her family group and joins another. She has her first foal at three or four years of age.

 **6** A young male zebra leaves his family group at about four years of age. He joins a bachelor herd for a time. Then he fights rival males to gather females of his own.

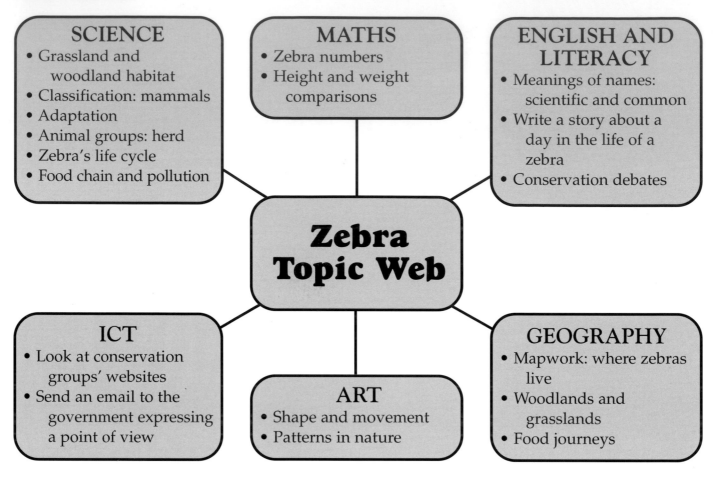

SCIENCE
- Grassland and woodland habitat
- Classification: mammals
- Adaptation
- Animal groups: herd
- Zebra's life cycle
- Food chain and pollution

MATHS
- Zebra numbers
- Height and weight comparisons

ENGLISH AND LITERACY
- Meanings of names: scientific and common
- Write a story about a day in the life of a zebra
- Conservation debates

Zebra Topic Web

ICT
- Look at conservation groups' websites
- Send an email to the government expressing a point of view

ART
- Shape and movement
- Patterns in nature

GEOGRAPHY
- Mapwork: where zebras live
- Woodlands and grasslands
- Food journeys

Extension Activities

English
- Debate whether zebras should be kept in zoos.
- Find and list collective names for groups of animals, or terms for their young eg calf, cub, chick.

Geography
- Trace a world map from an atlas. Show the location of Africa.
- Draw a zebra distribution map showing plains zebras, Grevy's zebras and mountain zebras.

Maths
- Use the zebra's head as a model for work on symmetry.

Art
- Make a grassland frieze, with zebras and other animals that share their habitat.

Science
- Make a display showing the ways in which zebras are adapted to their habitat.

Glossary

Bachelor A young male without a female partner.

Camouflage The colour or pattern of an animal that helps it to blend in with its surroundings.

Communal Used by a group rather than by an individual.

Extinct Died out completely; no longer alive anywhere.

Graze To eat grass and similar low-growing plants

Groom To take care of the skin and fur by removing pests, dirt and tangles.

Home range The area used by a group of animals, but not necessarily defended by them.

Hormones Chemical substances produced in the body that affect growth, breeding and behaviour.

Imprinting Following a particular individual animal, usually from birth.

Migration A regular long journey, usually in search of better conditions such as more food.

Predators Animals that kill and eat other animals.

Savannah Open, wooded country, with wide, grassy plains and scattered trees and bushes.

Territory An area which is controlled and defended by an animal or group.

Tropical At or near the Equator.

Ungulates Animals with hooves.

Weaned No longer relying on mother's milk, and able to survive on solid food.

Further Information

Organizations to Contact

WWF UK
Panda House, Weyside Park
Godalming, Surrey GU7 1XR
Tel: 01483 426444
Website: www.wwf-uk.org

International League for the Protection of Horses
Anne Colvin House
Snetterton
Norfolk NR16 2LP
ilph@ilph.org

Websites

www.animal-information.
com/text/zebra.html

www.africanconservation.
com/sheldrick2.html

www.bbc.co.uk/reallywild/
amazing/zebra.shtml

Books to Read

The Zebra: Striped Horse by Christine Denis-Huot (Charlesbridge Publishing, 1999)

Zebras: Striped Grass-Grazers by Lola M. Schaeffer (Capstone Press, 2001)

Zebras: Endangered by Shona Grimbly (Benchmark, 1998)

Quagga'a and Other Zebras by David Barnaby (Basset Publications, 1996)

Index

Page numbers in **bold** refer to photographs or illustrations.